# WE ARE ONE

Written and Illustrated by Melissa López Charepoo

First published 2020. Reprint 2026.

ISBN 978-1-971750-16-3 (paperback)

"Ye are the fruits of one tree, and the leaves of one branch. Deal ye one with another with the utmost love and harmony, with friendliness and fellowship. He Who is the Daystar of Truth beareth Me witness! So powerful is the light of unity that it can illuminate the whole earth."

-Bahá'u'lláh-

We are one humanity.

We are the
leaves of one
branch.

We are the
flowers of
one meadow.

We are the
lions of one
thicket.

We are the waves of one sea.

We are the fingers of one hand.

We are the birds of one garden.

We are the plants of one orchard.

We are one humanity.

We are the stars of one heaven.

We are the
grass of one
meadow.

We are the drops of one ocean.

We are the roses of one garden.

We are the rays of one sun.

We are the pearls of one ocean.

We are the fruits of one tree.

We are one humanity.

For further information about the Bahá'í Faith, please visit:

**www.bahai.org**

# References

"Ye are the fruits of one tree, and the leaves of one branch. Deal ye one with another with the utmost love and harmony, with friendliness and fellowship." - Bahá'u'lláh

"Ye are all the leaves of one tree and the drops of one ocean."- Bahá'u'lláh

"Be ye as the fingers of one hand, the members of one body." - Bahá'u'lláh

"These children are the plants of Thine orchard, the flowers of Thy meadow, the roses of Thy garden." - 'Abdu'l-Bahá

"O Thou Provider! The dearest wish of this servant of Thy Threshold is to behold the friends of east and west in close embrace; to see all the members of human society gathered with love in a single great assemblage, even as individual drops of water collected in one mighty sea; to behold them all as birds in one garden of roses, as pearls of one ocean, as leaves of one tree, as rays of one sun." - 'Abdu'l-Bahá

"May you become as the waves of one sea, stars of the same heaven, fruits adorning the same tree, roses of one garden in order that through you the oneness of humanity may establish its temple in the world of mankind, for you are the ones who are called to uplift the cause of unity among the nations of the earth." - 'Abdu'l-Bahá

"We must consider all as the leaves, branches and fruit of one tree, children of one household; for all are the progeny of Adam. We are waves of one sea, grass of the same meadow, stars in the same heaven; and we find shelter in the universal divine Protector." - 'Abdu'l-Bahá

"Ye are all the waves of one sea, the rays of one sun, the flowers of one garden, the lions of one thicket, the birds of one meadow, and the fragrant blossoms of one rose garden: wherefore ye are even as a single soul, and this letter is in reality written to each one of you." - 'Abdu'l-Bahá

## *Heartfelt Thanks to:*

My beloved husband Darioush Charepoo for all his support.

Our dearly loved boys for being the inspiration.

Leanna Guillén Mora for helping with proofreading and editing the book.

www.ingramcontent.com/pod-product-compliance
Ingram Content Group UK Ltd.
Pitfield, Milton Keynes, MK11 3LW, UK
UKHW060101300726
14090UKWH00003B/343

* 9 7 8 1 9 7 1 7 5 0 1 6 3 *